Dogs
in
Poetry

Dogs
in
Poetry

The ideal gift
for every dog-lover

TEMPUS

First published 2007

Tempus Publishing
Cirencester Road, Chalford
Stroud, Gloucestershire, GL6 8PE
www.tempus-publishing.com

Tempus Publishing is an imprint of NPI Media Group

© Tempus Publishing, 2007

The right of Tempus Publishing to be identified as the Author
of this work has been asserted in accordance with the
Copyrights, Designs and Patents Act 1988.

British Library Cataloguing in Publication Data.
A catalogue record for this book is available from the British Library.

ISBN 978 0 7524 4390 4

Typesetting and origination by NPI Media Group
Printed and bound in Great Britain

Contents

Treacherous Towser

There dwelt a farmer in the west,
As we're in story told;
Whose herds were large and flocks the best
That ever lined a fold.

Armed with a staff, his russet coat,
And Towser by his side—
Early and late he tuned his throat
And every wolf defied.

Loved Towser was his heart's delight,
In cringe and fawning skilled,
Entrusted with the flocks by night,
And guardian of the field.

'Towser,' quoth he, I'm for a fair;
Be regent in my room:
Pray of my tender flocks take care,
And keep all safe at home.

'I know thee watchful, just, and brave,
Right worthy such a place;
No wily fox shall thee deceive,
Nor wolf dare show his face.'

But ne'er did wolves a fold infest,
At regent Towser's rate:
He dined and supped upon the best,
And frequent breakfasts ate.

The farmer oft received advice,
And laughed at the report;
But, coming on him by surprise,
Just found him at the sport.

'Ungrateful beast,' quoth he, 'what means
That bloody mouth and paws?
I know the base, the treacherous stains,
Thy breach of trust and laws.

'The fruits of my past love I see;
Roger, the halter bring;
E'en truss him on that pippin-tree,
And let friend Towser swing.'

The Yelping Nuisance
of the Way

A village cur, of snappish race,
The pertest puppy of the place,
Imagined that his treble throat
Was blest with music's sweetest note;
In the mid road he basking lay,
The yelping nuisance of the way;
For not a creature passed along,
But had a sample of his song.
Soon as the trotting steed he hears,
He starts, he cocks his dapper ears;
Away he scours, assaults his hoof,
Now near him snarls, now barks aloof;
With shrill impertinence attends,
Nor leaves him till the village ends.
It chanced upon his evil day,
A Pad came pacing down the way;
The cur with never-ceasing tongue,
Upon the passing traveller sprung.
The horse, provoked from scorn to ire,

Flung backwards: rolling in the mire,
The puppy howled, and bleeding lay;
The Pad in peace pursued his way.
A shepherd's dog, who saw the deed,
Detesting the vexatious breed,
Bespoke him thus: 'When coxcombs prate,
They kindle wrath, contempt, or hate:
Thy teasing tongue had judgment tied,
Thou hadst not like a puppy died.'

The Meddling Mastiff

Those who in quarrels interpose
Must often wipe a bloody nose.

A mastiff, of true English blood,
Loved fighting better than his food.
When dogs were snarling for a bone,
He longed to make the war his own,
And often found (when two contend)
To interpose obtained his end.
He gloried in his limping pace;
The scars of honour seamed his face;
In ev'ry limb a gash appears,
And frequent fights retrenched his ears.
 As on a time he heard from far
Two dogs engaged in noisy war,
Away he scours and lays about him,
Resolved no fray should be without him.
Forth from his yard a tanner flies,
And to the bold intruder cries:
 'A cudgel shall correct your manners:

Whence sprang this cursed hate of tanners?
While on my clog you vent your spite,
Sirrah! 'tis me you dare not bite.'
To see the battle thus perplexed,
With equal rage a butcher, vexed,
Hoarse-screaming from the circled crowd
To the cursed mastiff cries aloud:

'Both Hockleyhole and Mary'bone
The combats of my dog have known:
He ne'er, like bullies coward-hearted,
Attacks in public to be parted.
Think not, rash fool, to share his fame;
Be his the honour—or the shame.'

Thus said, they swore, and raved like thunder,
Then dragged their fastened dogs asunder;
While clubs and kicks from every side
Rebounded from the mastiff's hide.
All reeking now with sweat and blood,
Awhile the parted warriors stood;
Then poured, upon the meddling foe,
Who, worried, howled and sprawled below.
He rose; and limping from the fray,
By both sides mangled, sneaked away.

The Turnspit Taught

'The dinner must be dished at one;
Where's this vexatious turnspit gone?
Unless the skulking cur is caught,
The sirloin's spoilt, and I'm in fault.'
Thus said (for sure you'll think it fit
That I the cook-maid's oaths omit),
With all the fury of a cook,
Her cooler kitchen Nan forsook:
The broom-stick o'er her head she waves,
She sweats, she stamps, she puffs, she raves
The sneaking cur before her flies;
She whistles, calls, fair speech she tries;
These nought avail. Her choler burns;

The fist and cudgel threat by turns.
With hasty stride she presses near;
He slinks aloof, and howls with fear.

   'Was ever cur so cursed (he cried)!
What star did at my birth preside!
Am I for life by compact bound
To tread the wheel's eternal round?
Inglorious task ! of all our race
No slave is half so mean and base.
Had fate a kinder lot assigned,
And formed me of the lap-dog kind,
I then, in higher life employed,
Had indolence and ease enjoyed;
And, like a gentleman, caressed,
Had been the lady's favourite guest;
Or were I sprung from spaniel line,
Was his sagacious nostril mine,
By me, their never-erring guide,
From wood and plain their feasts supplied,
Knights, squires, attendant on my pace,
Had shared the pleasures of the chase.'

   An ox by chance o'erheard his moan,
And thus rebuked the lazy drone:
'You by the duties of your post
Shall turn the spit when I'm the roast;
And for reward shall share the feast—
I mean shall pick my bones, at least.'

   Till now (th' astonished cur replies)
I looked on all with envious eyes...
Let envy then no more torment:

Think on the ox, and learn content.'
Thus said, close following at her heel,
With cheerful heart he mounts the wheel.

Argus

When wise Ulysses, from his native coast
Long kept by wars, and long by tempests tost,
Arrived at last—poor, old, disguised, alone,
To all his friends and ev'n his queen unknown,
Changed as he was, with age, and toils, and cares,
Furrowed his rev'rend face, and white his hairs,
In his own palace forced to ask his bread,
Scorned by those slaves his former bounty fed,
Forgot of all his own domestic crew,
His faithful dog his rightful master knew!
Unfed, unhoused, neglected, on the clay,
Like an old servant, now cashiered, he lay;
And though ev'n then expiring on the plain,
Touched with resentment of ungrateful man,
And longing to behold his ancient lord again.
Him when he saw, he rose, and crawled to meet,

('Twas all he could), and fawned, and kissed his feet,
  Seized with dumb joy; then falling by his side,
  Owned his returning lord, looked up, and died.

The Mad Dog

Goon people all, of every sort,
   Give ear unto my song,
And if you find it wondrous short—
   It cannot hold you long.

In Islington there was a man,
   Of whom the world might say:
That still a godly race he ran—
   Whene'er he went to pray.

A kind and gentle heart he had,
   To comfort friends and foes;
The naked every day he clad—
   When he put on his clothes.

And in that town a dog was found,
   As many dogs there be,
Both mongrel, puppy, whelp and hound,
   And curs of low degree.

This dog and man at first were friends;
    But when a pique began,
The dog, to gain some private ends,
    Went mad, and bit the man.

Around from all the neighbouring streets
    The wondering neighbours ran,
And swore the dog had lost his wits,
    To bite so good a man.

The wound it seemed both sore and sad
    To every Christian eye;
And while they swore the dog was mad,
    They swore the man would die.

But soon a wonder came to light,
    That showed the rogues they lied:
The man recovered of the bite—
    The dog it was that died.

Beau and the Water Lily

The noon was shady, and soft airs
    Swept Ouse's silent tide,
When 'scaped from literary cares,
    I wandered on his side.

My spaniel, prettiest of his race,
    And high in pedigree
(Two nymphs adorned with every grace.
    That spaniel found for me),

Now wantoned lost in flags and reeds,
    Now starting into sight,
Pursued the swallow o'er the meads,
    With scarce a slower flight.

It was the time that Ouse displayed
    His lilies newly blown;
Their beauties I intent surveyed,
    And one I wished my own.

With cane extended far I sought
  To steer it close to land;
But still the prize, though nearly caught,
  Escaped my eager hand.

Beau marked my unsuccessful pains
  With fixed considerate face,
And puzzling set his puppy brains
  To comprehend the case.

But with a chirrup clear and strong,
  Dispersing all his dream,
I thence withdrew, and followed long
  The windings of the stream.

My ramble ended, I returned;
  Beau, trotting far before,
The floating wreath again discerned,
  And, plunging, left the shore.

I saw him, with that lily cropped,
  Impatient swim to meet
My quick approach, and soon he dropped
  The treasure at my feet.

Charmed with the sight, 'The world,' I cried,
  'Shall hear of this thy deed:
My dog shall mortify the pride
  Of man's superior breed:

But chief myself I will enjoin,
    Awake at duty's call,
To show a love as prompt as thine,
    To Him who gives me all.'

Infallible Doussiekie

There was a wee bit wifukie was comin' frae the fair,
Had got a wee bit drappukie, that bred her meikle care,
It gaed about the wifie's heart, and she began to spew:
Oh ! quo' the wee wifukie, I wish I binna fou.
I wish I binna fou, quo' she, I wish I binna fou,
Oh! quo' the wee wifukie, I wish I binna fou.

If Johnnie find me barley-sick, I'm sure he'll claw my skin;
But I'll lie down and tak' a nap before that I gae in.
Sitting at the dyke-side, and taking o' her nap, By came a
packman laddie wi' a little pack,
Wi' a little pack, *etc.*

He's clippit a' her gowden locks, sae bonnie and sae lang,
He's ta'en her purse and a' her placks, and fast awa he ran;
And when the wifie wakened, her head was like a bee:
Oh! quo' the wee wifukie, this is nae me. This is nae me,
quo' she, this is nae me, Somebody has been felling me,
and this is nae me.

I have a little housikie, but and a kindly man;
A dog, they ca' him Doussiekie, if this be me he'll fawn.

The night was late, and dang out weet, and oh ! but it was
dark,
The doggie heard a body's foot, and he began to bark ;
Oh! when she heard the doggie bark, and kennin' it was he,
Oh ! weel ken ye, Doussie, quo' she, this is nae me,
This is nae me, *etc.*

The Miser's Only Friend

There watched a cur before the miser's gate—
A very cur, whom all men seemed to hate;
Gaunt, savage, shaggy, with an eye that shone
Like a live coal, and he possessed but one:
His bark was wild and eager, and became
That meagre body and that eye of flame;
His master prized him much, and Fang his name.
His master fed him largely; but not that,
Nor aught of kindness, made the snarler fat;
Flesh he devoured, but not a bit would stay—
He barked, and snarled, and growled it all away.
His ribs were seen extended like a rack,
And coarse red hair hung roughly o'er his back.
Lamed in one leg, and bruised in wars of yore,
Now his sore body made his temper sore.
Such was the friend of him who could not find,
Nor make him, one 'mong creatures of his kind.
Brave deeds of Fang his master often told,

The son of Fury, famed in deeds of old,
From Snatch and Rabid sprung; and noted they
In earlier times—each dog will have his day.

The notes of Fang were to his master known,
And dear—they bore some likeness to his own
For both conveyed to the experienced ear,
'I snarl and bite because I hate and fear.'
None passed ungreeted by the master's door,
Fang railed at all, but chiefly at the poor;
And when the nights were stormy, cold, and dark,
The act of Fang was a perpetual bark;
But though the master loved the growl of Fang,
There were who vowed the ugly cur to hang;
Whose angry master, watchful for his friend,
As strongly vowed his servant to defend.

In one dark night, and such as Fang before
Was ever known its tempests to outroar,
To his protector's wonder now expressed,
No angry notes—his anger was at rest.
The wond'ring master sought the silent yard,
Left Phoebe sleeping, and his door unbarred;
Nor more returned to that forsaken bed—
But lo! the morning came, and he was dead.
Fang and his master side by side were laid
In grim repose—their debt of nature paid.
The master's hand upon the cur's cold chest
Was now reclined, and had before been pressed,
As if he searched how deep and wide the wound

That laid such spirit in a sleep so sound;
And when he found it was the sleep of death,
A sympathising sorrow stopped his breath.
Close to his trusty servant he was found,
As cold his body, and his sleep as sound.

Beth Gelert

The spearman heard the bugle sound,
   And cheerly smiled the morn;
And many a brash, and many a hound,
   Obeyed Llewellyn's horn.

And still he blew a louder blast,
   And gave a louder cheer:
'Come, Gelert, come, wert never last
   Llewellyn's horn to hear !

Oh, where does faithful Gelert roam?
   The flower of all his race!
So true, so brave—a lamb at home,
   A lion in the chase!'

'Twas only at Llewellyn's board
   The faithful Gelert fed;
He watched, he served, he cheered his lord,
   And sentineled his bed.

In sooth, he was a peerless hound,
  The gift of Royal John;
But now no Gelert could be found,
  And all the chase rode on.

And now, as o'er the rocks and dells,
  The gallant chidings rise,
All Snowdon's craggy chaos yells
  With many-mingled cries.

That day Llewellyn little loved
  The chase of hart or hare;
And scant and small the booty proved,
  For Gelert was not there.

Unpleased Llewellyn homeward hied,
  When, near the portal-seat,
His truant, Gelert, he espied,
  Bounding his lord to greet.

But when he gained his castle-door,
  Aghast the chieftain stood;
The hound all o'er was smeared with gore
  His lips, his fangs ran blood!

Llewellyn gazed with fierce surprise,
  Unused such looks to meet,
His favourite checked his joyful guise,
  And crouched and licked his feet.

Onward in haste Llewellyn passed—
　　And on went Gelert too
And still, where'er his eyes were cast,
　　Fresh blood-gouts shocked his view!

O'erturned his infant's bed he found,
　　The bloodstained covert rent;
And all around, the walls and ground,
　　With recent blood besprent.

He called his child—no voice replied;
　　He searched—with terror wild.
Blood! blood! he found on every side,
　　But nowhere found the child!

Hell-hound! my child's by thee devoured!'
　　The frantic father cried;
And, to the hilt, his vengeful sword
　　He plunged in Gelert's side!

His suppliant looks, as prone he fell,
　　No pity could impart;
But still his Gelert's dying yell
　　Passed heavy o'er his heart.

Concealed beneath a tumbled heap,
　　His hurried search had missed,
All glowing from his rosy sleep,
　　The cherub-boy he kissed.

Nor scathe had he, nor harm, nor dread—
    But the same couch beneath
Lay a gaunt wolf, all torn and dead—
    Tremendous still in death!

Ah, what was then Llewllyn's pain,
    For now the truth was clear:
The gallant hound the wolf had slain,
    To save Llewellyn's heir.

Vain, vain was all Llewellyn's woe;
    'Best of thy kind, adieu!
The frantic deed which laid thee low
    This heart shall ever rue!'

And now a gallant tomb they raise,
    With costly sculpture decked;
And marbles, storied with his praise,
    Poor Gelert's bones protect.

Here never could the spearsman pass,
    Or forester, unmoved;
Here oft the tear-besprinkled grass
    Llewellyn's sorrow proved.

And here he hung his horn and spear;
    And there, as evening fell,
In fancy's ear he oft would hear
    Poor Gelert's dying yell.

And, till great Snowdon's rocks grow old,
    And cease the storm to brave.
The consecrated spot shall hold
    The name of 'Gelert's Grave.'

A Dog's Tragedy

On his morning rounds the Master
Goes to learn how all things fare;
Searches pasture after pasture,
Sheep and cattle eyes with care;
And, for silence or for talk,
He hath comrades in his walk;
Four dogs, each pair of different breed,
Distinguished two for scent, and two for speed.

See a hare before him started!
Off they fly in earnest chase;
Every dog is eager-hearted,
All the four are in the race:
And the hare whom they pursue
Knows from instinct what to do;
Her hope is near: no turn she makes;
But, like an arrow, to the river takes.

Deep the river was, and crusted
Thinly by a one night's frost;
But the nimble hare hath trusted
To the ice, and safely crost;
She hath crost, and without heed
All are following at full speed,
When, lo! the ice, so thinly spread,
Breaks—and the greyhound, Dart, is over head!

Better fate have Prince and Swallow—
See them cleaving to the sport!
Music has no heart to follow,
Little Music, she stops short.
She hath neither wish nor heart,
Hers is now another part:
A loving creature she, and brave!
And fondly strives her struggling friend to save.

From the brink her paws she stretches,
Very hands as you would say!
And afflicting moans she fetches,
As he breaks the ice away.
For herself she hath no fears,
Him alone she sees and hears,
Makes efforts with complainings; nor gives o'er
Until her fellow sinks to re-appear no more.

Fidelity

A barking sound the Shepherd hears,
A cry as of a dog or fox;
He halts—and searches with his eyes
Among the scattered rocks:
And now at distance can discern
A stirring in a brake of fern;
And instantly a dog is seen,
Glancing through that covert green.

The Dog is not of mountain breed;
Its motions, too, are wild and shy;
With something, as the Shepherd thinks,
Unusual in its cry:
Nor is there any one in sight
All round, in hollow or on height;
Nor shout, nor whistle strikes his ear;
What is the creature doing here?

It was a cove, a huge recess,
That keeps, till June, December's snow;
A lofty precipice in front,
A silent tarn below!
Far in the bosom of Helvellyn,
Remote from public road or dwelling,
Pathway, or cultivated land,
From trace of human foot or hand.

There sometimes doth a leaping fish
Send through the tarn a lonely cheer;
The crags repeat the raven's croak,
In symphony austere;
Thither the rainbow comes—the cloud
And mists that spread the flying shroud;
And sunbeams; and the sounding blast,
That, if it could, would hurry past;
But that enormous barrier holds it fast.

Not free from boding thoughts, a while
The Shepherd stood; then makes his way
O'er rocks and stones, following the Dog
As quickly as he may;
Nor far had gone before he found
A human skeleton on the ground;
The appalled Discoverer with a sigh
Looks round, to learn the history.

From those abrupt and perilous rocks
The Man had fallen, that place of fear!
At length upon the Shepherd's mind
It breaks, and all is clear:
He instantly recalled the name,
And who he was, and whence he came
Remembered, too, the very day
On which the Traveller passed this way.

But hear a wonder, for whose sake
This lamentable tale I tell!
A lasting monument of words
This wonder merits well.
The Dog, which still was hovering nigh,
Repeating the same timid cry,
This Dog had been through three months' space
A dweller in that savage place.

Yes, proof was plain that, since the day
When this ill-fated Traveller died,
The Dog had watched about the spot,
Or by his master's side
How nourished here through such long time
He knows, who gave that love sublime;
And gave that strength of feeling, great
Above all human estimate!

At the Siege of Corinth

He saw the lean dogs beneath the wall
Hold o'er the dead their carnival,
Gorging and growling o'er carcass and limb;
They were too busy to bark at him!
From a Tartar's skull they had stripped the flesh,
As ye peel the fig when its fruit is fresh;
And their white tusks crunched o'er the whiter skull,
As it slipped through their jaws, when their edge grew dull,
As they lazily mumbled the bones of the dead,
When they scarce could rise from the spot where they fed;
So well had they broken a lingering fast
With those who had fall'n for that night's repast.

Don Juan's Spaniel

A small old spaniel,—which had been Don Jose's,
  His father's, whom he loved, as ye may think,
For on such things the memory reposes
  With tenderness—stood howling on the brink,
Knowing (dogs have such intellectual noses!),
  No doubt, the vessel was about to sink;
And Juan caught him up, and ere he stepped
  Off, threw him in, and after him he leaped.

*   *   *   *

The fourth day came, but not a breath of air,
  And ocean slumbered like an unweaned child : The fifth
day, and their boat lay floating there ;
  The sea and sky were blue, and clear, and mild
With their one oar (I wish they had had a pair)
  What could they do ? And hunger's rage grew wild :
So Juan's spaniel, spite of his entreating,
  Was killed, and portioned out for present eating.

On the sixth day they fed upon his hide,
 And Juan, who had still refused because
The creature was his father's dog that died,
 Now feeling all the vulture in his jaws,
With some remorse received (though first denied)
 As a great favour one of the fore-paws,
Which he divided with Pedrillo, who
Devoured it, longing for the other too.

Tobias's Dog

Of the dog in ancient story
Many a pleasant tale is told;
As when young Tobias journeyed
To Ecbatane of old,

By the angel Raphael guided;
Went the faithful Dog and good,
Bounding through the Tigris meadows
Whilst they fished within the flood ;

Ate the crumbs which at the wedding
Fell upon 'taguel's floor ;
Barked for joy to see the cattle
Gathered for the bridal store;

Barked for joy when young Tobias,
With his bride and all her train,
And the money-bags from Media,
Left for Nineveh again.

And when Anna in the doorway
Stood to watch and wait for him,
Anxious mother! waiting, watching,
Till her eyes with tears were dim,

Saw she not the two men coming,
Young Tobias and his guide,
Hurrying on with their good tidings,
And the Dog was at their side!

They were coming dowered with blessings,
Like the Tigris' boundless flood,
And the Dog with joyous barking
Told the same as best he could.

The Fawning Whelp

The master Hunt, anon, foot-hot,
With his horn blew three mote
At the uncoupling of his hound is;
Within a while the hart found is,
Y-halloaed, and rechasèd fast
Long time, and so, at the last,
This hart roused and stole away
From all the hounds a privy way.
The hounds had overshot him all,
And were upon a default y-fall,
Therewith the Hunt wonder fast
Blew a forlorn at the last;
I was go walked from my tree,
And, as I went, there came by me
A whelp, that fawned me as I stood,
That had y-followed, and could no good;
It came and crept to me as low
Right as it had me y-know,
Held down his head, and joined his ears,

And laid all smooth down his hairs:
I would have caught it anon,
It fled, and was from me gone.

The Properties of a Good Greyhound

A greyhound should be headed like a Snake,
And necked like a Drake,
Footed like a Cat,
Tailed liked a Rat,

Sided like a Team,
Chined like a Beam.
The first year he must learn to feed,
The second year to field him lead,

The third year he is fellow-like,
The fourth year there is none sike,
The fifth year he is good enough,
The sixth year he shall hold the plough,

The seventh year he will avail
Great bitches for to assail,
The eighth year lick ladle,
The ninth year cart saddle,

And when he is comen to that year
Have him to the tanner,
For the best hound that ever bitch had
At nine year he is full bad.

Sunday Bear-Baiting

What folly is this, to keep with danger
A great mastiff dog, and a foul ugly bear?
And to this one end, to see them two fight
With terrible tearings—a foul ugly sight.
And yet methinks those men be most fools of all,
Whose store of money is but very small,
And yet every Sunday they will surely spend
One penny or two, the Bearward's living to mend.

At Paris Garden each Sunday a man shall not fail
To find two or three hundred for the Bearward's vale.
One halfpenny a piece they use for to give,
When some have not more in their purses, I believe.
Well, at the last day their conscience will declare
That the poor ought to have all that they may spare.
If you therefore it give to see a bear-fight, Be sure God his
curse upon you will light.

A New Point of View

Behold the feeble deer, what war they rage;
In timid breasts what baleful furies rage!
For death reciprocal each forehead bounds;
In mercy, feeling Caesar, send the hounds.

A Roman Tribute

But can you waft across the British tide
And land undangered on the further side,
O what great gains will certainly redound
From a free traffic in the British hound.

Mind not the badness of their forms or face—
That the sole blemish of the gen'rous race.
When the bold game turns back upon the spear,
And all the Furies wait upon the war,

First in the fight the whelps of Britain shine,
And snatch, Epirus, all the palm from thine.
Would you chase the deer,
Or urge the motions of the smaller hare,

Let the brisk greyhound of the Celtic name
Bound o'er the glebe and show his painted frame.
Swift as the wing that sails adown the wind,
Swift as the wish that darts along the mind,

The Celtic greyhound sweeps the level lea,
Eyes as he strains and stops the flying prey,
But should the game elude his watchful eyes
No nose sagacious tells him where it lies.

A Greek Compliment

A small bold breed, and steady to the game,
Next claims the tribute of peculiar fame,
Trained by the tribes on Britain's wildest shore,
Thence they their title of Agasses bore.
Small as the race that, useless to their lord,
Bask on the hearth, and beg about the board;
Crook-limbed, and black-eyed, all their frame appears
Flanked with no flesh, and bristled rough with hairs,
But shod each foot with hardest claws is seen
The sole's kind armour on the beaten green;
But fenced each jaw with closest teeth around,
And death sits instant on th' inflicted wound.
Far o'er the rest he quests the secret prey,
And sees each track wide opening to his ray:
Far o'er the rest he feels each scent that blows
Court the live nerve, and thrill along the nose.

The Deep-Toned Jowler

One hound alone has crossed the dreary height,
The deep-toned Jowler, ever staunch and true.
The chase was o'er...
The tents were reared, and fires of evening shone.
The mountain's sounds had perished in the gloom,
All save the unwearied Jowler's swelling tone,
That bore to trembling stag the sounds of doom,
While every cave of night rolled back the breathing boom.
The impassioned huntsman wended up the brae,
And loud the order of desistance bawled;
But ay, as louder waxed his tyrant's say,
Louder and fiercer, Jowler, unappalled,
Across the glen, along the mountain, brawled,
Unpractised he to part till blood was seen
Though sore by precipice and darkness galled,
He turned his dewlap to the starry sheen,
And howled in furious tone, with yelp and bay between.

*   *   *   *   *

54

There stood the monarch of the wild at bay
(The impetuous Jowler howling at his brow),
His cheeks all drenched with brine, his antlers grey,
Moving across the cliff; majestic, slow,
Like living fairy trees of blenched and leafless bough.
With ruthless shaft they pierced his heavy breast,
The baited, thirsty Jowler laps his blood;
The Royal hunter his brave hound caressed,
Lauded his zeal and spirit unsubdued;
While the staunch victor, of approval proud,
Rolled his brown back upon the prostrate slain,
Capered around in playful, whelpish mood,
As if unspent by all his toil and pain,
Then licked his crimson Hue, and looked to the hills again.

The Battlefield Staghounds

Yelled on the view the opening pack,
Rock, glen and cavern paid them back;
To many a mingled sound at once
The awakened mountains gave response.
A hundred dogs bayed deep and strong,
Clattered a hundred steeds along.
— Jaded now, and spent with toil,
Embossed with foam, and dark with soil,
While every gasp with sobs he drew,
The labouring stag strained full in view.
Two dogs of black Saint Hubert's breed,
Unmatched for courage, breath, and speed,
Fast on his flying traces came
And all but won that desperate game;
For scarce a spear's-length from his haunch
Vindictive toiled the bloodhounds staunch,
Nor nearer might the dogs attain,
Nor farther might the quarry strain.
Close on the hounds the hunter came

To cheer them on the vanished game.
Then through the dell his horn resounds,
From vain pursuit to call the hounds.
Back limped, with slow and crippled pace,
The sulky leaders of the chase;
Close to their master's side they pressed,
With drooping tail and humbled crest;
But still the dingle's hollow throat
Prolonged the swelling bugle-note.

The Teased Pet

The cow-boy still cuts short the day
By mingling mischief with his play;
Oft in the pond, with weeds o'ergrown,
Hurling quick the plashing stone
To cheat his dog, who watching lies,
And instant plunges for the prize;
And though each effort proves in vain,
He shakes his coat, and dives again,
Till, wearied with the fruitless play,
He drops his tail, and sneaks away.

The Dogs' Welcome

Don and Sancho, Tramp and Tray,
Upon the parlour steps collected,
Wagged all their tails, and seemed to say:
'Our master knows you; you're expected!'

Welcoming the Dawn

At morning's call
The small-voiced pug-dog welcomes in the sun,
And flea-bit mongrels, wakening one by one,
Give answer all.

The Pythagorean

Going abroad, he saw one day a hound was beaten
    sore;
Whereat his heart grew pitiful: 'Now beat the hound
    no more!
Give o'er thy cruel blows,' he cried; 'a man's soul
    verily
Is lodged in that same crouching beast—I know him
    by the cry.'

A Dumb Advocate

Nature that taught my silly dog, God wat,
Even for my sake to lick where I do love,
Enforced him, whereas my lady sat,
With humble suit before her falling flat,
As in his sort he might her pray and move
To rue upon his lord and not forget
The steadfast faith he beareth her, and love;
Kissing her hand: whom she could not remove
Away that would for frowning nor for threat,
As though he would have said in my behove,
Pity, my lord, your slave that doth remain,
Lest by his death you guiltless slay us twain.

The Brave Dog's Challenge

Vile cur, why will you late and soon
At honest people fly?
You, you, the veriest poltroon
Whene'er a wolf comes by!

Come on, and if your stomach be
So ravenous for a fight,
I'm ready! Try your teeth on me,
You'lll find that I bite.

For like Molossian mastiff stout,
Or dun Laconian hound,
That keeps sure ward, and sharp look-out
For all the sheepfolds round,

Through drifted snow with ears thrown back
I'm ready, night or day,
To follow fearless on the track
Of every beast of prey.

But you, when you have made wood
With bark and bellowing shake,
If any thief shall fling you food
The filthy bribe you take.

A Proud Boast

I never barked when out of season;
I never bit without a reason;
I ne'er insulted weaker brother;
Nor wronged by force or fraud another.
Though brutes are placed a rank below,
Happy for man could he say so!

Silent Echo

In wood and wild, ye warbling throng,
 Your heavy loss deplore;
Now, half extinct your powers of song,
 Sweet 'Echo' is no more.

Ye jarring, screeching things around,
 Scream yur discordant joys;
Now, half your din of tuneless sound
 With 'Echo' silent lies.

Maida

Beneath the sculptured form which late you wore,
Sleep soundly, Maida, at your master's door.

Exemplary Nick

Here lies poor Nick, an honest creature,
Of faithful, gentle, courteous nature;
A parlour pet unspoiled by favour,
A pattern of good dog behaviour.
Without a wish, without a dream,
Beyond his home and friends at Cheam,
Contentedly through life he trotted
Along the path that fate allotted;
Till time, his aged body wearing,
Bereaved him of his sight and hearing,
Then laid him down without a pain
To sleep, and never to awake again.

The Tumbler

The hound that men the Tumbler name,
When he hare or coney doth espy,
Doth seem another way his course to frame,
As though he meant not to approach more nigh,
But yet he meeteth at the last his game,
And shaketh it until he make it die.

Rival Favourites

Huntsmen, I charge thee, tender well my hounds:
Trash Merrimen,—the poor cur is embossed;
And couple Clowder with the deep-mouthed brach.
Saw'st thou not, boy, how Silver made it good
At the hedge-corner, in the coldest fault?
I would not lose the dog for twenty pound.

The Bear-Baiting Cur

Oft have I seen a hot o'erweening cur
Run back and bite, because he was withheld;
Who, being suffered with the bear's fell paw,
Hath clapped his tail between his legs and cried.

The Uses of the Dog

Nor last, forget thy faithful dogs; but feed
With fattening whey the mastiff's generous breed,
And Spartan race; who, for the fold's relief,
Will prosecute with cries the nightly thief;
Repulse the prowling wolf, and hold at bay
The mountain robbers, rushing to the prey;
With cries of hounds thou may'st pursue the fear
Of flying hares, and chase the fallow deer;
Rouse from thier desert dens the bristled rage
Of boars, and beamy stags in toils engage.

Bull-Baiting

A yet ignobler band is guarded round
With dogs of war—the spurning bull their prize;
And now he bellows, humbled to the ground,
And now they sprawl in howlings to the skies.

Finn and Ossian Hunting

Finn and Oshin went out to hunt,
Fal lal loo as fal lal la!
With a noble train of men and dogs,
Not less in number than a hundred men,
So swift of foot and keen, none were their like;
With scores of bandogs fierce they sallied forth
O'er hill and dale much havoc for to make.
Whom they left at home but youthful Orree!
Who slept secure beneath the shadowy rock.
Full threescore greyhounds with their whelps they left,
As many old dames to attend the young.

Epitaph on a Spaniel

Here rest the relics of a friend below,
Blest with more sense than half the folks I know;
Fond of his ease and to no parties prone,
He damned no sect, but calmly gnawed his bone;
Performed his functions well in every way,—
Blush, Christians, if you can, and copy Tray.

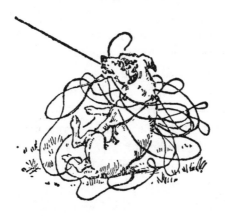

Fleet Marmion

Farewell! a long farewell to thee,
The fleetest, bravest hound
That ever coursed on hill or lea,
Or swept the heathy ground;
Foremost, whatever dog was there,
My Marmion! slayer of the hare!

Farewell! a long farewell to thee,
The fondest, dearest, best,
That ever played around my knee,
Or leaped upon my breast;
By all beloved, and loving all,
My Marmion! favourite, of the hall!

Thou diedst when Fame's bright wreath was nearest
On IIsley's dreary heath;
I should have sung thy triumph, dearest,
And not have mourned thy death;

Most cherished in that parting hour
Which showed thy love's undying power!

Who dreamed of death that gazed on thee?
Thy light and golden form,
Skimming along the meadowy sea,
A sunbeam in the storm!
From air and fire derived, thy birth
Had nought to do with drossy earth!

With spirit dancing in thine eye,
Love brooding in thy breast,
Gay as the flower-fed butterfly,
Calm as the turtle's nest;
Free from the care, the thought of man,
Bliss crowned thy being's little span.

And loved in life, and mourned in death,
Upon thy simple bier
The rose and myrtle's fragrant breath Blend with
affection's tear:
And proudly verdant laurels wave
Their branches o'er my Marmion's grave.

And long thy memory shall live,
And long thy well-earned fame,
And oft a sigh shall coursers give
At thy remembered name;
And long thy mistress' heart shall tell
The sadness of her last farewell!

The Cynotaph

Poor Tray Charmant!
Poor Tray de noon ami!

Oh! where shall I bury my poor dog Tray,
Now his fleeting breath has passed away?
Seventeen years, I can venture to say,
Have I seen him gambol, and frolic, and play,
Ever more happy, and frisky, and gay,
As though every one of his months was May,
And the whole of his life one long holiday
Now he's a lifeless lump of clay,
Oh! where shall I bury my faithful Tray?
I am almost tempted to think it hard
That it may not be there, in yon sunny churchyard
Where the green willows wave
O'er the peaceful grave,
Which holds all that once was honest and brave,
Kind and courteous, and faithful, and true;
Qualities, Tray, that were found in you.
But it may not be—you sacred ground,

By holiest feelings fenced around,
May ne'er within its hallowed bound
Receive the dust of a soulless hound.
I would not place him in yonder fine,
Where the mid-day sun through the storied pane
Throws on the pavement a crimson stain;

No!—Tray's humble tomb would look but shabby
'Mid the sculptured shrines of that gorgeous Abbey.
Besides, in the place
They say there's not space
To bury what wet-nurses call 'a Babby.'
Even 'Rarelien Jonson,' that famous wight,
I am told, is interred there bolt upright,
In just such a posture, beneath his bust,
As Tray used to sit in to beg for a crust.
The epitaph, too,
Would scarcely do:
For what could it say but 'Here lies Tray,
A very good dog of a kind in his day'?

I would not place him beneath thy walls,
And proud o'ershadowing dome, St. Paul's!
No, Tray, we must yield,
And go further a-field;
To lay you by Nelson were downright effront'ry;
—We'll be off from the city, and look at the country.
It shall not be there,
In that sepulchred square,
Where folks are interred for the sake of the air.

(Though, pay but the dues, they could hardly refuse
To Tray what they grant to Thugs and Hindoos,
Turks, Infidels, Heretics, Jumpers and Jews.)

Nor shall he be laid
By that cross Old Maid,
Miss Penelope Bird,—of whom it is said
All the dogs in the parish were ever afraid.
No,—if Tray were interred
By Penelope Bird,
No dog would be e'er so be- 'whelp'ed and be- 'cur'ed—
All the night long her cantankerous Sprite
Would be running about in the pale moonlight,
Chasing him round, and attempting to lick
The ghost of poor Tray with the ghost of a stick.

Stay!—let me see!—Ay—here it shall be,
At the root of the gnarled and time-worn tree,
Where Tray and I
Would often lie,
And watch the bright clouds as they floated by
In the broad expanse of the clear blue sky,
When the sun was bidding the world good-bye;
And the plaintive nightingale, warbling nigh,
Ponied forth her mournful, melody;
While the tender wood-pigeon's cooing cry
Has made me say to myself, with a sigh,
'How nice you would eat with a steak in a pie!'
Ay, here it shall be! far, far from the view
Of the noisy world and its maddening crew.

Simple and few,
Tender and true
The lines o'er his grave.—They have, some of them, too,
The advantage of being remarkably new.

EPITAPH
Affliction sore
Long time he bore,
Physicians were in vain!
Grown blind, alas! he'd
Some prussic acid,
And that put him out of his pain!

Boatswain, His One Friend

When some proud son of man returns to earth,
Unknown to glory, but upheld by birth,
The sculptor's art exhausts the pomp of woe,
And storied urns record who rests below;
When all is done, upon the tomb is seen,
Not what he was, but what he should have been:
But the poor dog, in life the firmest friend,
The first to welcome, foremost to defend,

Whose honest heart is still his roaster's own,
Who labours, fights, lives, breathes for him alone,
Unhonoured falls, unnoticed all his worth,
Denied in heaven the soul he held on earth:
While man, vain insect! hopes to be forgiven,
And claims himself a sole, exclusive heaven.
O man! thou feeble tenant of an hour,
Debased by slavery, or corrupt by power,
Who knows thee well must chit thee with disgust,
Degraded mass of animated dust!

Thy love is lust, thy friendship all a cheat,
Thy smiles hypocrisy, thy words deceit!
By nature vile, ennobled but by name,
Each kindred brute might bid thee blush for shame.
Ye ! who, perchance, behold this simple urn,
Pass on—it honours none you wish to mourn
To mark a friend's remains these stones arise;
I never knew but one, and here he lies.

The Drowned Spaniel

The day-long bluster of the storm was o'er,
The sands were bright; the winds had fallen asleep,
And, from the far horizon, o'er the deep
The sunset swam unshadowed to the shore.

High up, the rainbow had not passed away,
When, roving o'er the shingle beach, I found
A little waif, a spaniel newly drowned;
The shining waters kissed him as he lay.

In some kind heart thy gentle memory dwells,
I said, and, though thy latest aspect tells
Of drowning pains and mortal agony,
Thy master's self might weep and smile to see
His little dog stretched on these rosy shells,
Betwixt the rainbow and the rosy sea.

Louis

No cold philosophy nor cynic sneer
Checks the unbidden and the honest tear;
What little difference and how short the span
Betwixt thy instinct and the mind of man!

On an Irish Retriever

Ten years of loving loyalty
Unthanked should not go to earth,
And I, who had no less from thee,
Devote this tribute to thy worth.

For thou didst give to me, old friend,
Thy service while thy life did last;
Thy life and service have an end,
And here I thank thee for the past.

Trusted and faithful, tried and true,
Watchful and swift to do my will,
Grateful for care that was thy due,
To duty's call obedient still.

From ill thou knew'st thou didst refrain,
The good thou knew'st thou strove to do,
Nor dream of fame, nor greed of gain,
Man's keenest, spurs urged thee thereto.

Brute, with a heart of human love,
And speechless soul of instinct, fine!
How few by reason's law who move
Deserve an epitaph like thine!

A Spark Divine

Not hopeless, round this calm sepulchral spot,
A wreath presaging life we twine;
If God he love, what sleeps below was not
Without a spark divine.

Kaiser Dead

What, Kaiser dead ? The heavy news
Post-haste to Cobham calls the Muse,
From where in Farringford she brews
    The ode sublime,
Or with Pen-bryn's bold bard pursues
    A rival rhyme.

Kai's bracelet tail, Kai's busy feet,
Were known to all the village street.
'What, poor Kai dead?' say all I meet;
    'A loss indeed!'
O for the croon pathetic, sweet,
    Of Robin's reed!

Six years ago I brought him down,
A baby dog, from London town
Round his small throat of black and brown
    A ribbon blue,

And vouched by glorious renown
    A dachshound true.

His mother, most majestic dame,
Of blood unmixed, from Potsdam came;
And Kaiser's race we deemed the same
    No lineage higher.
And so he bore the imperial name.
    But ah, his sire!

Soon, soon the days conviction bring.
The collie hair, the collie swing,
The tail's indomitable ring,
    The eye's unrest—
The case was clear; a mongrel thing
    Kai stood confest.

But all those virtues, which commend
The humbler sort who serve and tend,
Were thine in store, thou faithful friend.
    What sense, what cheer!
To us, declining tow'rds our end,
    A mate how dear!

Thine eye was bright, thy coat it shone;
Thou hadst thine errands, off and on;
In joy thy last morn flew; anon,
    A fit! All's over;
And thou art gone where Geist hath gone,
    And Toss, and Rover.

Islet the Dachs

Our Islet out of Helgoland, dismissed
From his quaint tenement, quits hates and loves.
There lived with us a wagging humourist
In that hound's arch dwarf-legged on boxing gloves.

Questions

Where are you now, little wandering
Life, that so faithfully dwelt with us,
Played with us, fed with us, felt with us,
Years we grew fonder and fonder in?

You who but yesterday sprang to us,
Are we for ever bereft of you?
And is this all that is left of you—
One little grave, and a pang to us?

On some Elegies
on a Lap-Dog

Poor dog, whom rival poets strive
To celebrate in plaintive strains;
If thou hadst howled so when alive.
Thou hadst been beaten for thy pains.

Illustrations

Illustrations on pages 5, 10, 29 and 57 are reproduced courtesy of Pascal J. Barry.

The perfect partner to Dogs in Poetry!

Cats
in
Poetry

Discover new sides to your household cat within these elegantly composed
sonnets, limericks and odes. As an animal often considered 'part of the family',
Cats in Poetry justly honours the important role cats have in millions of
people's lives.

ISBN 978 07524 4432 1
£9.99